Before I Go

A LITTLE GUIDE TO GOING
ON WITHOUT ME.
FILLED WITH LOVE AND
ADVICE, SO I'LL ALWAYS
BE THERE IF
YOU NEED ME.

Before I Go...
Published by
Verna Scott-Culkin.
Copyright © 2016
Verna Scott-Culkin.

ISBN 978-1-5262-0468-4

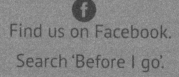

Find us on Facebook.

Search 'Before I go'.

More 'Before...' books
available soon.

Book design by Giles Culkin
www.gilesculkin.com

FROM

_____

TO

_____

● ● ●

MY WISHES FOR YOU ALL:

NAME:

NAME:

NAME:

NAME:

NAME:

NAME:

NAME:

NAME:

NAME:

NAME:

MY WISHES FOR YOU ALL:

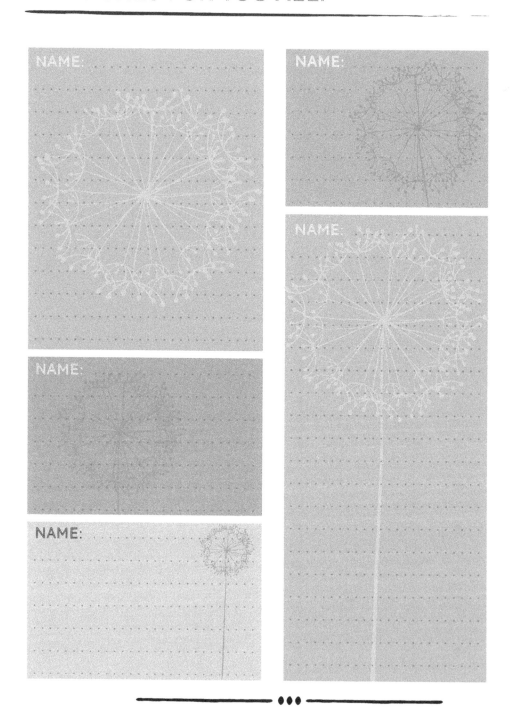

NAME:

NAME:

NAME:

NAME:

NAME:

NAME:

NAME:

NAME:

NAME:

NAME:

MY WISHES FOR YOU ALL:

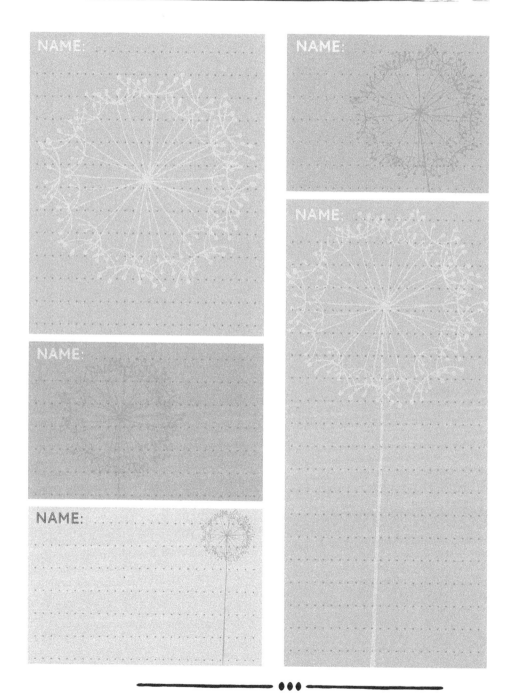

NAME:

NAME:

NAME:

NAME:

NAME:

NAME:

NAME:

NAME:

NAME:

NAME:

MY WISHES FOR YOU ALL:

NAME:

NAME:

NAME:

NAME:

NAME:

NAME:

NAME:

NAME:

NAME:

NAME:

MY WISHES FOR YOU ALL:

NAME:

NAME:

NAME:

NAME:

NAME:

NAME:

NAME:

NAME:

NAME:

NAME:

HAPPY MEMORIES

HAPPY MEMORIES

HAPPY MEMORIES

HAPPY MEMORIES

RECIPES

FAVOURITE RECIPES TO SHARE, COPY & ENJOY. IF YOU DON'T HAVE 'FOOD' RECIPES HOW ABOUT THE RECIPE TO A HAPPY LIFE, GOOD RELATIONSHIP OR ANYTHING ELSE

FAVOURITE RECIPES TO SHARE, COPY & ENJOY. IF YOU DON'T HAVE 'FOOD' RECIPES HOW ABOUT THE RECIPE TO A HAPPY LIFE, GOOD RELATIONSHIP OR ANYTHING ELSE

RECIPES

FAVOURITE RECIPES TO SHARE, COPY & ENJOY. IF YOU DON'T HAVE 'FOOD'
RECIPES HOW ABOUT THE RECIPE TO A HAPPY LIFE, GOOD RELATIONSHIP
OR ANYTHING ELSE

FAVOURITE RECIPES TO SHARE, COPY & ENJOY. IF YOU DON'T HAVE 'FOOD'
RECIPES HOW ABOUT THE RECIPE TO A HAPPY LIFE, GOOD RELATIONSHIP
OR ANYTHING ELSE

RECIPES

FAVOURITE RECIPES TO SHARE, COPY & ENJOY. IF YOU DON'T HAVE 'FOOD' RECIPES HOW ABOUT THE RECIPE TO A HAPPY LIFE, GOOD RELATIONSHIP OR ANYTHING ELSE

FAVOURITE RECIPES TO SHARE, COPY & ENJOY. IF YOU DON'T HAVE 'FOOD' RECIPES HOW ABOUT THE RECIPE TO A HAPPY LIFE, GOOD RELATIONSHIP OR ANYTHING ELSE

RECIPES

FAVOURITE RECIPES TO SHARE, COPY & ENJOY. IF YOU DON'T HAVE 'FOOD'
RECIPES HOW ABOUT THE RECIPE TO A HAPPY LIFE, GOOD RELATIONSHIP
OR ANYTHING ELSE

FAVOURITE RECIPES TO SHARE, COPY & ENJOY. IF YOU DON'T HAVE 'FOOD' RECIPES HOW ABOUT THE RECIPE TO A HAPPY LIFE, GOOD RELATIONSHIP OR ANYTHING ELSE

RECIPES

FAVOURITE RECIPES TO SHARE, COPY & ENJOY. IF YOU DON'T HAVE 'FOOD' RECIPES HOW ABOUT THE RECIPE TO A HAPPY LIFE, GOOD RELATIONSHIP OR ANYTHING ELSE

FAVOURITE RECIPES TO SHARE, COPY & ENJOY. IF YOU DON'T HAVE 'FOOD' RECIPES HOW ABOUT THE RECIPE TO A HAPPY LIFE, GOOD RELATIONSHIP OR ANYTHING ELSE

WISE WORDS

SOME ADVICE ON VARIOUS SUBJECTS (IT'S MY BOOK AND FINALLY YOU HAVE
TO LISTEN TO MY WORDS OF WISDOM) ARE YOU SITTING COMFORTABLY?

WISE WORDS

SOME ADVICE ON VARIOUS SUBJECTS (IT'S MY BOOK AND FINALLY YOU HAVE
TO LISTEN TO MY WORDS OF WISDOM) ARE YOU SITTING COMFORTABLY?

. . . .
. . . .
. . . .
. . . .
. . . .
. . . .
. . . .
. . . .
. . . .
. . . .
. . . .
. . . .
. . . .
. . . .
. . . .
. . . .
. . . .
. . . .
. . . .
. . . .
. . . .
. . . .
. . . .
. . . .
. . . .

—————————— ●●● ——————————

WISE WORDS

SOME ADVICE ON VARIOUS SUBJECTS (IT'S MY BOOK AND FINALLY YOU HAVE TO LISTEN TO MY WORDS OF WISDOM) ARE YOU SITTING COMFORTABLY?

WISE WORDS

SOME ADVICE ON VARIOUS SUBJECTS (IT'S MY BOOK AND FINALLY YOU HAVE
TO LISTEN TO MY WORDS OF WISDOM) ARE YOU SITTING COMFORTABLY?

WISE WORDS

SOME ADVICE ON VARIOUS SUBJECTS (IT'S MY BOOK AND FINALLY YOU HAVE
TO LISTEN TO MY WORDS OF WISDOM) ARE YOU SITTING COMFORTABLY?

· ·
· ·
· ·
· ·
· ·
· ·
· ·
· ·
· ·
· ·
· ·
· ·
· ·
· ·
· ·
· ·
· ·
· ·
· ·
· ·
· ·
· ·
· ·

———— ●●● ————

PLACES SPECIAL TO ME

PLACES SPECIAL TO ME

PLACES SPECIAL TO ME

FAVOURITE FILMS & WHEN TO WATCH THEM

FAVOURITE FILMS & WHEN TO WATCH THEM

FAVOURITE FILMS & WHEN TO WATCH THEM

FAVOURITE POEMS, SONGS OR SAYINGS

FAVOURITE POEMS, SONGS OR SAYINGS

FAVOURITE POEMS, SONGS OR SAYINGS

CONTACTS

CONTACTS FOR PEOPLE SPECIAL TO ME THAT YOU MAY NOT HAVE.

NAME: ....
ADDRESS: ....
....
....
PHONE: ....
EMAIL: ....

NAME: ....
ADDRESS: ....
....
....
PHONE: ....
EMAIL: ....

NAME: ....
ADDRESS: ....
....
....
PHONE: ....
EMAIL: ....

NAME: ....
ADDRESS: ....
....
....
PHONE: ....
EMAIL: ....

NAME: . . . .
ADDRESS: . . . .

. . . .

. . . .
PHONE: . . . .
EMAIL: . . . .

NAME: . . . .
ADDRESS: . . . .

. . . .

. . . .
PHONE: . . . .
EMAIL: . . . .

NAME: . . . .
ADDRESS: . . . .

. . . .

. . . .
PHONE: . . . .
EMAIL: . . . .

NAME: . . . .
ADDRESS: . . . .

. . . .

. . . .
PHONE: . . . .
EMAIL: . . . .

● ● ●

CONTACTS

CONTACTS FOR PEOPLE SPECIAL TO ME THAT YOU MAY NOT HAVE.

NAME: . . . .
ADDRESS: . . . .
. . . .
. . . .
PHONE: . . . .
EMAIL: . . . .

NAME: . . . .
ADDRESS: . . . .
. . . .
. . . .
PHONE: . . . .
EMAIL: . . . .

NAME: . . . .
ADDRESS: . . . .
. . . .
. . . .
PHONE: . . . .
EMAIL: . . . .

NAME: . . . .
ADDRESS: . . . .
. . . .
. . . .
PHONE: . . . .
EMAIL: . . . .

NAME: . . . .
ADDRESS: . . . .
. . . .
. . . .
PHONE: . . . .
EMAIL: . . . .

NAME: . . . .
ADDRESS: . . . .
. . . .
. . . .
PHONE: . . . .
EMAIL: . . . .

NAME: . . . .
ADDRESS: . . . .
. . . .
. . . .
PHONE: . . . .
EMAIL: . . . .

NAME: . . . .
ADDRESS: . . . .
. . . .
. . . .
PHONE: . . . .
EMAIL: . . . .

CONTACTS

CONTACTS FOR PEOPLE SPECIAL TO ME THAT YOU MAY NOT HAVE.

NAME: ....

ADDRESS: ....

....

....

PHONE: ....

EMAIL: ....

NAME: ....

ADDRESS: ....

....

....

PHONE: ....

EMAIL: ....

NAME: ....

ADDRESS: ....

....

....

PHONE: ....

EMAIL: ....

NAME: ....

ADDRESS: ....

....

....

PHONE: ....

EMAIL: ....

NAME: . . . .
ADDRESS: . . . .
. . . .
. . . .
PHONE: . . . .
EMAIL: . . . .

NAME: . . . .
ADDRESS: . . . .
. . . .
. . . .
PHONE: . . . .
EMAIL: . . . .

NAME: . . . .
ADDRESS: . . . .
. . . .
. . . .
PHONE: . . . .
EMAIL: . . . .

NAME: . . . .
ADDRESS: . . . .
. . . .
. . . .
PHONE: . . . .
EMAIL: . . . .

CONTACTS

CONTACTS FOR PEOPLE SPECIAL TO ME THAT YOU MAY NOT HAVE.

NAME: . . . .
ADDRESS: . . . .
. . . .
. . . .
PHONE: . . . .
EMAIL: . . . .

NAME: . . . .
ADDRESS: . . . .
. . . .
. . . .
PHONE: . . . .
EMAIL: . . . .

NAME: . . . .
ADDRESS: . . . .
. . . .
. . . .
PHONE: . . . .
EMAIL: . . . .

NAME: . . . .
ADDRESS: . . . .
. . . .
. . . .
PHONE: . . . .
EMAIL: . . . .

NAME: . . . .
ADDRESS: . . . .

. . . .

. . . .
PHONE: . . . .
EMAIL: . . . .

NAME: . . . .
ADDRESS: . . . .

. . . .

. . . .
PHONE: . . . .
EMAIL: . . . .

NAME: . . . .
ADDRESS: . . . .

. . . .

. . . .
PHONE: . . . .
EMAIL: . . . .

NAME: . . . .
ADDRESS: . . . .

. . . .

. . . .
PHONE: . . . .
EMAIL: . . . .

●●●

CONTACTS

CONTACTS FOR PEOPLE SPECIAL TO ME THAT YOU MAY NOT HAVE.

NAME: . . . .
ADDRESS: . . . .
. . . .
. . . .
PHONE: . . . .
EMAIL: . . . .

NAME: . . . .
ADDRESS: . . . .
. . . .
. . . .
PHONE: . . . .
EMAIL: . . . .

NAME: . . . .
ADDRESS: . . . .
. . . .
. . . .
PHONE: . . . .
EMAIL: . . . .

NAME: . . . .
ADDRESS: . . . .
. . . .
. . . .
PHONE: . . . .
EMAIL: . . . .

NAME: . . . .
ADDRESS: . . . .
. . . .
. . . .
PHONE: . . . .
EMAIL: . . . .

NAME: . . . .
ADDRESS: . . . .
. . . .
. . . .
PHONE: . . . .
EMAIL: . . . .

NAME: . . . .
ADDRESS: . . . .
. . . .
. . . .
PHONE: . . . .
EMAIL: . . . .

NAME: . . . .
ADDRESS: . . . .
. . . .
. . . .
PHONE: . . . .
EMAIL: . . . .

BIRTHDAYS I'D LIKE YOU TO REMEMBER

FAMILY & FRIENDS, NEAREST & DEAREST.

JANUARY

WHO. . . . . WHEN. . . . .
WHO. . . . . WHEN. . . . .
WHO. . . . . WHEN. . . . .
WHO. . . . . WHEN. . . . .
WHO. . . . . WHEN. . . . .
WHO. . . . . WHEN. . . . .
WHO. . . . . WHEN. . . . .

FEBRUARY

WHO. . . . . WHEN. . . . .
WHO. . . . . WHEN. . . . .
WHO. . . . . WHEN. . . . .
WHO. . . . . WHEN. . . . .
WHO. . . . . WHEN. . . . .
WHO. . . . . WHEN. . . . .
WHO. . . . . WHEN. . . . .

MARCH

WHO. . . . . WHEN. . . . .
WHO. . . . . WHEN. . . . .
WHO. . . . . WHEN. . . . .
WHO. . . . . WHEN. . . . .
WHO. . . . . WHEN. . . . .
WHO. . . . . WHEN. . . . .
WHO. . . . . WHEN. . . . .

•••

APRIL

WHO . . . .   WHEN . . . .
WHO . . . .   WHEN . . . .
WHO . . . .   WHEN . . . .
WHO . . . .   WHEN . . . .
WHO . . . .   WHEN . . . .
WHO . . . .   WHEN . . . .
WHO . . . .   WHEN . . . .

MAY

WHO . . . .   WHEN . . . .
WHO . . . .   WHEN . . . .
WHO . . . .   WHEN . . . .
WHO . . . .   WHEN . . . .
WHO . . . .   WHEN . . . .
WHO . . . .   WHEN . . . .
WHO . . . .   WHEN . . . .

JUNE

WHO . . . .   WHEN . . . .
WHO . . . .   WHEN . . . .
WHO . . . .   WHEN . . . .
WHO . . . .   WHEN . . . .
WHO . . . .   WHEN . . . .
WHO . . . .   WHEN . . . .
WHO . . . .   WHEN . . . .

BIRTHDAYS I'D LIKE YOU TO REMEMBER

FAMILY & FRIENDS, NEAREST & DEAREST.

JULY

WHO. . . . .   WHEN. . . . .
WHO. . . . .   WHEN. . . . .
WHO. . . . .   WHEN. . . . .
WHO. . . . .   WHEN. . . . .
WHO. . . . .   WHEN. . . . .
WHO. . . . .   WHEN. . . . .
WHO. . . . .   WHEN. . . . .

AUGUST

WHO. . . . .   WHEN. . . . .
WHO. . . . .   WHEN. . . . .
WHO. . . . .   WHEN. . . . .
WHO. . . . .   WHEN. . . . .
WHO. . . . .   WHEN. . . . .
WHO. . . . .   WHEN. . . . .
WHO. . . . .   WHEN. . . . .

SEPTEMBER

WHO. . . . .   WHEN. . . . .
WHO. . . . .   WHEN. . . . .
WHO. . . . .   WHEN. . . . .
WHO. . . . .   WHEN. . . . .
WHO. . . . .   WHEN. . . . .
WHO. . . . .   WHEN. . . . .
WHO. . . . .   WHEN. . . . .

●●●

OCTOBER

WHO . . . . WHEN . . . .
WHO . . . . WHEN . . . .
WHO . . . . WHEN . . . .
WHO . . . . WHEN . . . .
WHO . . . . WHEN . . . .
WHO . . . . WHEN . . . .
WHO . . . . WHEN . . . .

NOVEMBER

WHO . . . . WHEN . . . .
WHO . . . . WHEN . . . .
WHO . . . . WHEN . . . .
WHO . . . . WHEN . . . .
WHO . . . . WHEN . . . .
WHO . . . . WHEN . . . .
WHO . . . . WHEN . . . .

DECEMBER

WHO . . . . WHEN . . . .
WHO . . . . WHEN . . . .
WHO . . . . WHEN . . . .
WHO . . . . WHEN . . . .
WHO . . . . WHEN . . . .
WHO . . . . WHEN . . . .
WHO . . . . WHEN . . . .

FINANCES*

BANK ACCOUNTS

BANK: . . . .
ADDRESS: . . . .
. . . .
DETAILS: . . . .
. . . .
. . . .

BANK: . . . .
ADDRESS: . . . .
. . . .
DETAILS:. . . . .
. . . .
. . . .

BANK: . . . .
ADDRESS: . . . .
. . . .
DETAILS:. . . . .
. . . .
. . . .

BANK: . . . .
ADDRESS:. . . . .
. . . .
DETAILS: . . . .
. . . .
. . . .

*YOU CAN'T TAKE IT WITH YOU.

SHARES & BONDS

NAME: . . . .
AMOUNT: . . . .
DETAILS: . . . .
. . . .

NAME: . . . .
AMOUNT: . . . .
DETAILS: . . . .
. . . .

NAME: . . . .
AMOUNT: . . . .
DETAILS: . . . .
. . . .

NAME: . . . .
AMOUNT: . . . .
DETAILS: . . . .
. . . .

NAME: . . . .
AMOUNT: . . . .
DETAILS: . . . .
. . . .

FINANCES

INSURANCE POLICIES

TYPE: . . . .
COMPANY: . . . .
POLICY N°: . . . .
DETAILS: . . . .
. . . .

TYPE: . . . .
COMPANY: . . . .
POLICY N°: . . . .
DETAILS: . . . .
. . . .

TYPE: . . . .
COMPANY: . . . .
POLICY N°: . . . .
DETAILS: . . . .
. . . .

TYPE: . . . .
COMPANY: . . . .
POLICY N°: . . . .
DETAILS: . . . .
. . . .

TYPE: . . . .
COMPANY: . . . .
POLICY N°: . . . .
DETAILS: . . . .

LATEST WILL

NAME: . . . .

COMPANY :. . . . .

DETAILS: . . . .

. . . .

ANYTHING ELSE

. . . .

. . . .

. . . .

. . . .

. . . .

. . . .

. . . .

. . . .

. . . .

. . . .

. . . .

. . . .

. . . .

. . . .

. . . .

. . . .

. . . .

. . . .

. . . .

. . . .

. . . .

MILESTONES TO CELEBRATE

WHETHER IT'S RAISING A GLASS, SITTING QUIETLY OR DANCING THE
NIGHT AWAY, THESE ARE SOME THINGS I'D LIKE YOU TO CELEBRATE

DATE:. . . . .
OCCASION:. . . . .
. . . .
. . . .
. . . .

DATE:. . . . .
OCCASION:. . . . .
. . . .
. . . .
. . . .

DATE:. . . . .
OCCASION:. . . . .
. . . .
. . . .
. . . .

DATE:. . . . .
OCCASION:. . . . .
. . . .
. . . .
. . . .

DATE:...
OCCASION:...
....
....
....
....

DATE:...
OCCASION:...
....
....
....
....

DATE:...
OCCASION:...
....
....
....
....

DATE:...
OCCASION:...
....
....
....

MILESTONES TO CELEBRATE

WHETHER IT'S RAISING A GLASS, SITTING QUIETLY OR DANCING THE
NIGHT AWAY, THESE ARE SOME THINGS I'D LIKE YOU TO CELEBRATE

DATE:..
OCCASION:...
....
....
....

DATE:..
OCCASION:...
....
....
....

DATE:..
OCCASION:...
....
....
....

DATE:..
OCCASION:...
....
....
....

DATE:...
OCCASION:...
....
....
....

DATE:...
OCCASION:...
....
....
....

DATE:...
OCCASION:...
....
....
....

DATE:...
OCCASION:...
....
....
....

MILESTONES TO CELEBRATE

WHETHER IT'S RAISING A GLASS, SITTING QUIETLY OR DANCING THE
NIGHT AWAY, THESE ARE SOME THINGS I'D LIKE YOU TO CELEBRATE

DATE:. . . . .
OCCASION:. . . . .
. . . .
. . . .
. . . .

DATE:. . . . .
OCCASION:. . . . .
. . . .
. . . .
. . . .

DATE:. . . . .
OCCASION:. . . . .
. . . .
. . . .
. . . .

DATE:. . . . .
OCCASION:. . . . .
. . . .
. . . .
. . . .

DATE: . . . .
OCCASION: . . . .
. . . .
. . . .
. . . .

DATE: . . . .
OCCASION: . . . .
. . . .
. . . .
. . . .

DATE: . . . .
OCCASION: . . . .
. . . .
. . . .
. . . .

DATE: . . . .
OCCASION: . . . .
. . . .
. . . .
. . . .

SPECIAL THINGS TO CHERISH

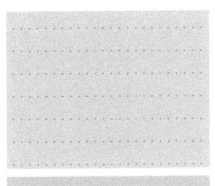

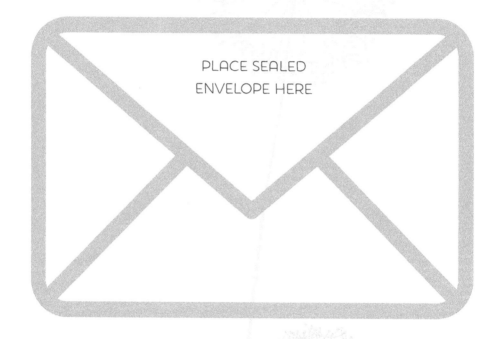

PLACE SEALED
ENVELOPE HERE

A FEW THANKYOUs

A FEW THANKYOUs

· ·
· ·
· ·
· ·
· ·
· ·
· ·
· ·
· ·
· ·
· ·
· ·
· ·
· ·
· ·
· ·
· ·
· ·
· ·
· ·
· ·
· ·
· ·
· ·
· ·

—— —— • • • —— ——

A FEW THANKYOUs

AFTER I'VE GONE

AFTER I'VE GONE

AFTER I'VE GONE

FURTHER THOUGHTS

FURTHER THOUGHTS

FURTHER THOUGHTS

Before I Go

BY VERNA SCOTT-CULKIN

A UNIQUE JOURNAL 'YOU' CREATE

So, if you knew you were leaving loved ones behind (for any reason) what would you want to tell them? What would you want to pass on, to share? What would you want them to know about you that maybe you never said?

If we all had the chance wouldn't we all choose to leave this world and our loved ones with some of our invaluable advice and musings?

BEFORE I GO is a personal journal allowing you to pass on the little pieces of the jigsaw puzzle that make up the *IRREPLACEABLE* you.

Fill it with all the things that matter to you.

Fill it in privately or with everyone's knowledge. Record your thoughts and wishes for your family and friends, creating a personal memory book as you go.

Write, Stick or even Staple extra pages in, it's YOUR book – make it your own – messy or pristine.

With pages to fill in, ranging from 'Wise Words' to 'Favourite Songs, Poems' and 'Films' and 'Wishes For Your Family' to 'Milestones to Celebrate', there's even a space for a sealed 'My Send Off' envelope.

So whether you have a lifetime or a short time, you could fill in this Personal journal and pass it on when the time comes, so when you leave this world, your loved ones hearts are a little less heavy and the chair 'round the table a little less empty.

THE STORY BEHIND BEFORE I GO...

Having lost my Father to Cancer and Mother-in-law to Alzheimer's, we now have two very empty chairs around the dinner table at our lovely and regular family get togethers.

Around the same time one of my closest friends was diagnosed with Breast Cancer.

She was a busy mum of two young kids, working, running the house and I wondered what would happen if she wasn't there anymore?

Yes life would go on, her husband would cope, people would help, the kids would grow up but what if there was a guide to 'her' that she could leave behind (she was a lucky one and she made a full recovery, but many don't).

So, me and my husband talked about a book that could be filled with love, advice, wishes and even recipes – something my dad may have filled in privately and my mother in law could have filled in on her 'good' days and my friend, just to fill in and take control of something when her world felt it was collapsing around her.

We couldn't find another book like it, a book that the reader fills in to then pass on when the time came, SO we created one – somehow I'm now a swimming teacher, publisher and author!

So many people, when they leave this world, take all their thoughts, hopes, sayings and wishes with them – maybe we should all have 'THAT' conversation and start putting pen to paper.

Far from being morbid, we would like to think that your journal will be full of love, memories, thoughts and wishes. A unique book to leave your family and friends. Truly made with love.

The secret of my Chewy Chocolate Fudge Brownies and recipe are going in my book for future generations to enjoy.

Contact Us

Email – Beforejournals@gmail.com
Website – http://beforejournals.wixsite.com/beforeigo
Facebook – Search Before I Go or @beforejournals
Twitter – BeforeJournals
Instagram – beforejournals

#haveyouhadthatconversation

Printed in the USA
CPSIA information can be obtained
at www.ICGtesting.com
LVHW062139120923
758043LV00008B/40